Name

Address

Home

Work

Cell

Email

Notes

Name

Address

Home Work

Cell Email

Notes

Name

Address

Home Work

Cell Email

Notes

Name

Address

Home Work

Cell Email

Notes

Name

Address

Home Work

Cell Email

Notes

Name

Address

Home Work

Cell Email

Notes

Name

Address

Home Work

Cell Email

Notes

Name

Address

Home Work

Cell Email

Notes

Name

Address

Home Work

Cell Email

Notes

Name

Address

Home Work

Cell Email

Notes

Name

Address

Home Work

Cell Email

Notes

Name

Address

Home Work

Cell Email

Notes

Name

Address

Home Work

Cell Email

Notes

Name

Address

Home Work

Cell Email

Notes

Name

Address

Home Work

Cell Email

Notes

Name

Address

Home Work

Cell Email

Notes

Name

Address

Home Work

Cell Email

Notes

Name

Address

Home Work

Cell Email

Notes

Name

Address

Home Work

Cell Email

Notes

Name

Address

Home Work

Cell Email

Notes

Name

Address

Home Work

Cell Email

Notes

Name

Address

Home Work

Cell Email

Notes

Name

Address

Home Work

Cell Email

Notes

Name

Address

Home Work

Cell Email

Notes

Name

Address

Home Work

Cell Email

Notes

Name

Address

Home | Work

Cell | Email

Notes

Name

Address

Home | Work

Cell | Email

Notes

Name

Address

Home | Work

Cell | Email

Notes

Name

Address

Home | Work

Cell | Email

Notes

Name

Address

Home Work

Cell Email

Notes

Name

Address

Home Work

Cell Email

Notes

Name

Address

Home Work

Cell Email

Notes

Name

Address

Home Work

Cell Email

Notes

Name

Address

Home | Work

Cell | Email

Notes

Name

Address

Home | Work

Cell | Email

Notes

Name

Address

Home | Work

Cell | Email

Notes

Name

Address

Home | Work

Cell | Email

Notes

Name

Address

Home Work

Cell Email

Notes

Name

Address

Home Work

Cell Email

Notes

Name

Address

Home Work

Cell Email

Notes

Name

Address

Home Work

Cell Email

Notes

Name

Address

Home Work

Cell Email

Notes

Name

Address

Home Work

Cell Email

Notes

Name

Address

Home Work

Cell Email

Notes

Name

Address

Home Work

Cell Email

Notes

Name

Address

Home Work

Cell Email

Notes

Name

Address

Home Work

Cell Email

Notes

Name

Address

Home Work

Cell Email

Notes

Name

Address

Home Work

Cell Email

Notes

Name

Address

Home Work

Cell Email

Notes

Name

Address

Home Work

Cell Email

Notes

Name

Address

Home Work

Cell Email

Notes

Name

Address

Home Work

Cell Email

Notes

Name

Address

Home Work

Cell Email

Notes

Name

Address

Home Work

Cell Email

Notes

Name

Address

Home Work

Cell Email

Notes

Name

Address

Home Work

Cell Email

Notes

Name

Address

Home Work

Cell Email

Notes

Name

Address

Home Work

Cell Email

Notes

Name

Address

Home Work

Cell Email

Notes

Name

Address

Home Work

Cell Email

Notes

D

Name

Address

Home Work

Cell Email

Notes

Name

Address

Home Work

Cell Email

Notes

Name

Address

Home Work

Cell Email

Notes

Name

Address

Home Work

Cell Email

Notes

Name

Address

Home Work

Cell Email

Notes

Name

Address

Home Work

Cell Email

Notes

Name

Address

Home Work

Cell Email

Notes

Name

Address

Home Work

Cell Email

Notes

Name

Address

Home Work

Cell Email

Notes

Name

Address

Home Work

Cell Email

Notes

Name

Address

Home Work

Cell Email

Notes

Name

Address

Home Work

Cell Email

Notes

Name

Address

Home Work

Cell Email

Notes

Name

Address

Home Work

Cell Email

Notes

Name

Address

Home Work

Cell Email

Notes

Name

Address

Home Work

Cell Email

Notes

Name

Address

Home Work

Cell Email

Notes

Name

Address

Home Work

Cell Email

Notes

Name

Address

Home Work

Cell Email

Notes

Name

Address

Home Work

Cell Email

Notes

Name

Address

Home Work

Cell Email

Notes

Name

Address

Home Work

Cell Email

Notes

Name

Address

Home Work

Cell Email

Notes

Name

Address

Home Work

Cell Email

Notes

Name

Address

Home Work

Cell Email

Notes

Name

Address

Home Work

Cell Email

Notes

Name

Address

Home Work

Cell Email

Notes

Name

Address

Home Work

Cell Email

Notes

Name

Address

Home Work

Cell Email

Notes

Name

Address

Home Work

Cell Email

Notes

Name

Address

Home Work

Cell Email

Notes

Name

Address

Home Work

Cell Email

Notes

Name

Address

Home Work

Cell Email

Notes

Name

Address

Home Work

Cell Email

Notes

Name

Address

Home Work

Cell Email

Notes

Name

Address

Home Work

Cell Email

Notes

Name
Address

Home Work
Cell Email
Notes

Name
Address

Home Work
Cell Email
Notes

Name
Address

Home Work
Cell Email
Notes

Name
Address

Home Work
Cell Email
Notes

Name

Address

Home Work

Cell Email

Notes

Name

Address

Home Work

Cell Email

Notes

Name

Address

Home Work

Cell Email

Notes

Name

Address

Home Work

Cell Email

Notes

Name

Address

Home Work

Cell Email

Notes

Name

Address

Home Work

Cell Email

Notes

Name

Address

Home Work

Cell Email

Notes

Name

Address

Home Work

Cell Email

Notes

Name

Address

Home Work

Cell Email

Notes

Name

Address

Home Work

Cell Email

Notes

Name

Address

Home Work

Cell Email

Notes

Name

Address

Home Work

Cell Email

Notes

Name

Address

Home Work

Cell Email

Notes

Name

Address

Home Work

Cell Email

Notes

Name

Address

Home Work

Cell Email

Notes

Name

Address

Home Work

Cell Email

Notes

Name

Address

Home Work

Cell Email

Notes

Name

Address

Home Work

Cell Email

Notes

Name

Address

Home Work

Cell Email

Notes

Name

Address

Home Work

Cell Email

Notes

Name
Address

Home Work
Cell Email
Notes

Name
Address

Home Work
Cell Email
Notes

Name
Address

Home Work
Cell Email
Notes

Name
Address

Home Work
Cell Email
Notes

Name

Address

Home Work

Cell Email

Notes

Name

Address

Home Work

Cell Email

Notes

Name

Address

Home Work

Cell Email

Notes

Name

Address

Home Work

Cell Email

Notes

Name

Address

Home Work

Cell Email

Notes

Name

Address

Home Work

Cell Email

Notes

Name

Address

Home Work

Cell Email

Notes

Name

Address

Home Work

Cell Email

Notes

Name

Address

Home Work

Cell Email

Notes

Name

Address

Home Work

Cell Email

Notes

Name

Address

Home Work

Cell Email

Notes

Name

Address

Home Work

Cell Email

Notes

Name

Address

Home Work

Cell Email

Notes

Name

Address

Home Work

Cell Email

Notes

Name

Address

Home Work

Cell Email

Notes

Name

Address

Home Work

Cell Email

Notes

Name

Address

Home Work

Cell Email

Notes

Name

Address

Home Work

Cell Email

Notes

Name

Address

Home Work

Cell Email

Notes

Name

Address

Home Work

Cell Email

Notes

Name

Address

Home Work

Cell Email

Notes

Name

Address

Home Work

Cell Email

Notes

Name

Address

Home Work

Cell Email

Notes

Name

Address

Home Work

Cell Email

Notes

Name

Address

Home Work

Cell Email

Notes

Name

Address

Home Work

Cell Email

Notes

Name

Address

Home Work

Cell Email

Notes

Name

Address

Home Work

Cell Email

Notes

Name

Address

Home Work

Cell Email

Notes

Name

Address

Home Work

Cell Email

Notes

Name

Address

Home Work

Cell Email

Notes

Name

Address

Home Work

Cell Email

Notes

Name

Address

Home Work

Cell Email

Notes

Name

Address

Home Work

Cell Email

Notes

Name

Address

Home Work

Cell Email

Notes

Name

Address

Home Work

Cell Email

Notes

Name

Address

Home Work

Cell Email

Notes

Name

Address

Home Work

Cell Email

Notes

Name

Address

Home Work

Cell Email

Notes

Name

Address

Home Work

Cell Email

Notes

Name

Address

Home Work

Cell Email

Notes

Name

Address

Home Work

Cell Email

Notes

Name

Address

Home Work

Cell Email

Notes

Name

Address

Home Work

Cell Email

Notes

Name

Address

Home Work

Cell Email

Notes

Name

Address

Home Work

Cell Email

Notes

Name

Address

Home Work

Cell Email

Notes

Name

Address

Home Work

Cell Email

Notes

Name

Address

Home Work

Cell Email

Notes

Name

Address

Home Work

Cell Email

Notes

Name

Address

Home Work

Cell Email

Notes

Name

Address

Home Work

Cell Email

Notes

Name

Address

Home Work

Cell Email

Notes

Name

Address

Home Work

Cell Email

Notes

Name

Address

Home Work

Cell Email

Notes

Name

Address

Home Work

Cell Email

Notes

Name

Address

Home Work

Cell Email

Notes

Name

Address

Home Work

Cell Email

Notes

Name

Address

Home Work

Cell Email

Notes

Name

Address

Home Work

Cell Email

Notes

Name

Address

Home Work

Cell Email

Notes

Name

Address

Home Work

Cell Email

Notes

Name

Address

Home Work

Cell Email

Notes

Name

Address

Home Work

Cell Email

Notes

Name

Address

Home Work

Cell Email

Notes

Name

Address

Home Work

Cell Email

Notes

Name

Address

Home Work

Cell Email

Notes

Name

Address

Home Work

Cell Email

Notes

Name

Address

Home Work

Cell Email

Notes

Name

Address

Home Work

Cell Email

Notes

Name

Address

Home Work

Cell Email

Notes

Name

Address

Home Work

Cell Email

Notes

Name

Address

Home Work

Cell Email

Notes

Name

Address

Home Work

Cell Email

Notes

Name

Address

Home Work

Cell Email

Notes

Name

Address

Home Work

Cell Email

Notes

Name

Address

Home Work

Cell Email

Notes

Name

Address

Home Work

Cell Email

Notes

Name

Address

Home Work

Cell Email

Notes

Name

Address

Home Work

Cell Email

Notes

Name

Address

Home Work

Cell Email

Notes

Name

Address

Home Work

Cell Email

Notes

Name

Address

Home Work

Cell Email

Notes

Name

Address

Home Work

Cell Email

Notes

Name

Address

Home Work

Cell Email

Notes

Name

Address

Home Work

Cell Email

Notes

Name

Address

Home Work

Cell Email

Notes

Name

Address

Home Work

Cell Email

Notes

Name

Address

Home Work

Cell Email

Notes

Name

Address

Home Work

Cell Email

Notes

Name

Address

Home Work

Cell Email

Notes

Name

Address

Home Work

Cell Email

Notes

Name
Address

Home Work
Cell Email
Notes

Name
Address

Home Work
Cell Email
Notes

Name
Address

Home Work
Cell Email
Notes

Name
Address

Home Work
Cell Email
Notes

Name

Address

Home Work

Cell Email

Notes

Name

Address

Home Work

Cell Email

Notes

Name

Address

Home Work

Cell Email

Notes

Name

Address

Home Work

Cell Email

Notes

Name

Address

Home Work

Cell Email

Notes

Name

Address

Home Work

Cell Email

Notes

Name

Address

Home Work

Cell Email

Notes

Name

Address

Home Work

Cell Email

Notes

Name

Address

Home Work

Cell Email

Notes

Name

Address

Home Work

Cell Email

Notes

Name

Address

Home Work

Cell Email

Notes

Name

Address

Home Work

Cell Email

Notes

Name

Address

Home Work

Cell Email

Notes

Name

Address

Home Work

Cell Email

Notes

Name

Address

Home Work

Cell Email

Notes

Name

Address

Home Work

Cell Email

Notes

Name

Address

Home Work

Cell Email

Notes

Name

Address

Home Work

Cell Email

Notes

Name

Address

Home Work

Cell Email

Notes

Name

Address

Home Work

Cell Email

Notes

Name
Address

Home Work
Cell Email
Notes

Name
Address

Home Work
Cell Email
Notes

Name
Address

Home Work
Cell Email
Notes

Name
Address

Home Work
Cell Email
Notes

Name

Address

Home Work

Cell Email

Notes

Name

Address

Home Work

Cell Email

Notes

Name

Address

Home Work

Cell Email

Notes

Name

Address

Home Work

Cell Email

Notes

Name

Address

Home Work

Cell Email

Notes

Name

Address

Home Work

Cell Email

Notes

Name

Address

Home Work

Cell Email

Notes

Name

Address

Home Work

Cell Email

Notes

Name

Address

Home Work

Cell Email

Notes

Name

Address

Home Work

Cell Email

Notes

Name

Address

Home Work

Cell Email

Notes

Name

Address

Home Work

Cell Email

Notes

Name

Address

Home Work

Cell Email

Notes

Name

Address

Home Work

Cell Email

Notes

Name

Address

Home Work

Cell Email

Notes

Name

Address

Home Work

Cell Email

Notes

Name

Address

Home Work

Cell Email

Notes

Name

Address

Home Work

Cell Email

Notes

Name

Address

Home Work

Cell Email

Notes

Name

Address

Home Work

Cell Email

Notes

Name

Address

Home Work

Cell Email

Notes

Name

Address

Home Work

Cell Email

Notes

Name

Address

Home Work

Cell Email

Notes

Name

Address

Home Work

Cell Email

Notes

Name

Address

Home Work

Cell Email

Notes

Name

Address

Home Work

Cell Email

Notes

Name

Address

Home Work

Cell Email

Notes

Name

Address

Home Work

Cell Email

Notes

Name

Address

Home Work

Cell Email

Notes

Name

Address

Home Work

Cell Email

Notes

Name

Address

Home Work

Cell Email

Notes

Name

Address

Home Work

Cell Email

Notes

Name
Address

Home Work
Cell Email
Notes

Name
Address

Home Work
Cell Email
Notes

Name
Address

Home Work
Cell Email
Notes

Name
Address

Home Work
Cell Email
Notes

Name

Address

Home Work

Cell Email

Notes

Name

Address

Home Work

Cell Email

Notes

Name

Address

Home Work

Cell Email

Notes

Name

Address

Home Work

Cell Email

Notes

Name

Address

Home Work

Cell Email

Notes

Name

Address

Home Work

Cell Email

Notes

Name

Address

Home Work

Cell Email

Notes

Name

Address

Home Work

Cell Email

Notes

Name

Address

Home Work

Cell Email

Notes

Name

Address

Home Work

Cell Email

Notes

Name

Address

Home Work

Cell Email

Notes

Name

Address

Home Work

Cell Email

Notes

P

Name

Address

Home Work

Cell Email

Notes

Name

Address

Home Work

Cell Email

Notes

Name

Address

Home Work

Cell Email

Notes

Name

Address

Home Work

Cell Email

Notes

Name

Address

Home Work

Cell Email

Notes

Name

Address

Home Work

Cell Email

Notes

Name

Address

Home Work

Cell Email

Notes

Name

Address

Home Work

Cell Email

Notes

Name

Address

Home Work

Cell Email

Notes

Name

Address

Home Work

Cell Email

Notes

Name

Address

Home Work

Cell Email

Notes

Name

Address

Home Work

Cell Email

Notes

Name

Address

Home Work

Cell Email

Notes

Name

Address

Home Work

Cell Email

Notes

Name

Address

Home Work

Cell Email

Notes

Name

Address

Home Work

Cell Email

Notes

Name

Address

Home Work

Cell Email

Notes

Name

Address

Home Work

Cell Email

Notes

Name

Address

Home Work

Cell Email

Notes

Name

Address

Home Work

Cell Email

Notes

Name
Address

Home Work
Cell Email
Notes

Name
Address

Home Work
Cell Email
Notes

Name
Address

Home Work
Cell Email
Notes

Name
Address

Home Work
Cell Email
Notes

Name

Address

Home Work

Cell Email

Notes

Name

Address

Home Work

Cell Email

Notes

Name

Address

Home Work

Cell Email

Notes

Name

Address

Home Work

Cell Email

Notes

Name

Address

Home Work

Cell Email

Notes

Name

Address

Home Work

Cell Email

Notes

Name

Address

Home Work

Cell Email

Notes

Name

Address

Home Work

Cell Email

Notes

Name

Address

Home Work

Cell Email

Notes

Name

Address

Home Work

Cell Email

Notes

Name

Address

Home Work

Cell Email

Notes

Name

Address

Home Work

Cell Email

Notes

Name

Address

Home | Work

Cell | Email

Notes

Name

Address

Home | Work

Cell | Email

Notes

Name

Address

Home | Work

Cell | Email

Notes

Name

Address

Home | Work

Cell | Email

Notes

Name

Address

Home Work

Cell Email

Notes

Name

Address

Home Work

Cell Email

Notes

Name

Address

Home Work

Cell Email

Notes

Name

Address

Home Work

Cell Email

Notes

Name

Address

Home Work

Cell Email

Notes

Name

Address

Home Work

Cell Email

Notes

Name

Address

Home Work

Cell Email

Notes

Name

Address

Home Work

Cell Email

Notes

Name

Address

Home Work

Cell Email

Notes

Name

Address

Home Work

Cell Email

Notes

Name

Address

Home Work

Cell Email

Notes

Name

Address

Home Work

Cell Email

Notes

Name

Address

Home Work

Cell Email

Notes

Name

Address

Home Work

Cell Email

Notes

Name

Address

Home Work

Cell Email

Notes

Name

Address

Home Work

Cell Email

Notes

Name

Address

Home Work

Cell Email

Notes

Name

Address

Home Work

Cell Email

Notes

Name

Address

Home Work

Cell Email

Notes

Name

Address

Home Work

Cell Email

Notes

Name

Address

Home Work

Cell Email

Notes

Name

Address

Home Work

Cell Email

Notes

Name

Address

Home Work

Cell Email

Notes

Name

Address

Home Work

Cell Email

Notes

Name

Address

Home Work

Cell Email

Notes

Name

Address

Home Work

Cell Email

Notes

Name

Address

Home Work

Cell Email

Notes

Name

Address

Home Work

Cell Email

Notes

Name

Address

Home Work

Cell Email

Notes

Name

Address

Home Work

Cell Email

Notes

Name

Address

Home Work

Cell Email

Notes

Name

Address

Home Work

Cell Email

Notes

Name

Address

Home Work

Cell Email

Notes

Name

Address

Home Work

Cell Email

Notes

Name

Address

Home Work

Cell Email

Notes

Name

Address

Home Work

Cell Email

Notes

Name

Address

Home Work

Cell Email

Notes

Name

Address

Home Work

Cell Email

Notes

Name

Address

Home Work

Cell Email

Notes

Name

Address

Home Work

Cell Email

Notes

Name
Address

Home Work
Cell Email
Notes

Name
Address

Home Work
Cell Email
Notes

Name
Address

Home Work
Cell Email
Notes

Name
Address

Home Work
Cell Email
Notes

Name

Address

Home Work

Cell Email

Notes

Name

Address

Home Work

Cell Email

Notes

Name

Address

Home Work

Cell Email

Notes

Name

Address

Home Work

Cell Email

Notes

Name

Address

Home Work

Cell Email

Notes

Name

Address

Home Work

Cell Email

Notes

Name

Address

Home Work

Cell Email

Notes

Name

Address

Home Work

Cell Email

Notes

Name

Address

Home Work

Cell Email

Notes

Name

Address

Home Work

Cell Email

Notes

Name

Address

Home Work

Cell Email

Notes

Name

Address

Home Work

Cell Email

Notes

Name

Address

Home Work

Cell Email

Notes

Name

Address

Home Work

Cell Email

Notes

Name

Address

Home Work

Cell Email

Notes

Name

Address

Home Work

Cell Email

Notes

Name

Address

Home Work

Cell Email

Notes

Name

Address

Home Work

Cell Email

Notes

Name

Address

Home Work

Cell Email

Notes

Name

Address

Home Work

Cell Email

Notes

Name

Address

Home Work

Cell Email

Notes

Name

Address

Home Work

Cell Email

Notes

Name

Address

Home Work

Cell Email

Notes

Name

Address

Home Work

Cell Email

Notes

Name

Address

Home Work

Cell Email

Notes

Name

Address

Home Work

Cell Email

Notes

Name

Address

Home Work

Cell Email

Notes

Name

Address

Home Work

Cell Email

Notes

Name

Address

Home Work

Cell Email

Notes

Name

Address

Home Work

Cell Email

Notes

Name

Address

Home Work

Cell Email

Notes

Name

Address

Home Work

Cell Email

Notes

Name

Address

Home Work

Cell Email

Notes

Name

Address

Home Work

Cell Email

Notes

Name

Address

Home Work

Cell Email

Notes

Name

Address

Home Work

Cell Email

Notes

Name

Address

Home Work

Cell Email

Notes

Name

Address

Home Work

Cell Email

Notes

Name

Address

Home Work

Cell Email

Notes

Name

Address

Home Work

Cell Email

Notes

Name

Address

Home Work

Cell Email

Notes

Name

Address

Home Work

Cell Email

Notes

Name

Address

Home Work

Cell Email

Notes

Name

Address

Home Work

Cell Email

Notes

Name

Address

Home Work

Cell Email

Notes

Name

Address

Home Work

Cell Email

Notes

Name

Address

Home Work

Cell Email

Notes

Name

Address

Home Work

Cell Email

Notes

Name

Address

Home Work

Cell Email

Notes

Name

Address

Home Work

Cell Email

Notes

Name

Address

Home Work

Cell Email

Notes

Name

Address

Home Work

Cell Email

Notes

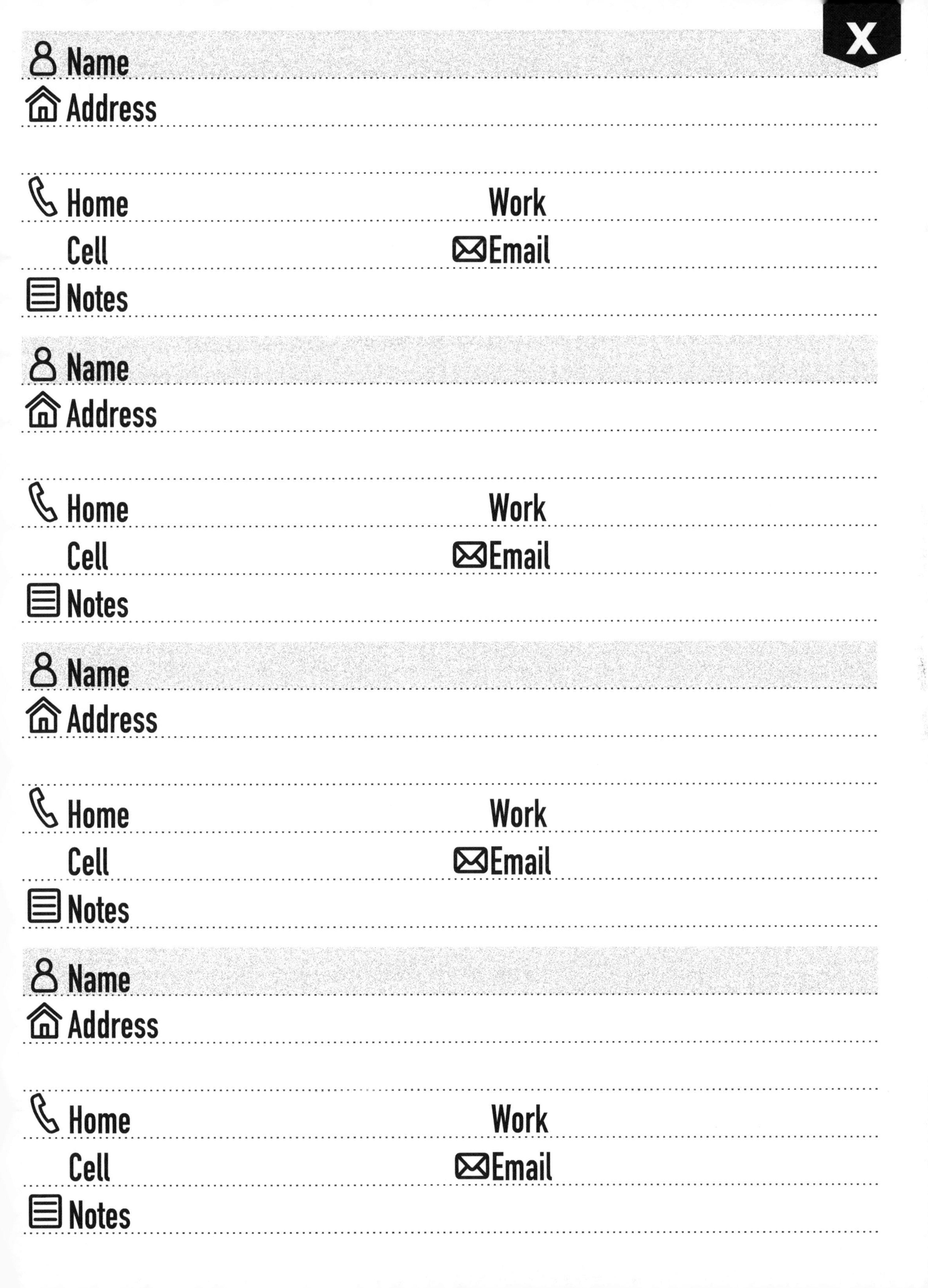
X
Name
Address
Home
Work
Cell
Email
Notes
Name
Address
Home
Work
Cell
Email
Notes
Name
Address
Home
Work
Cell
Email
Notes
Name
Address
Home
Work
Cell
Email
Notes

Name

Address

Home Work

Cell Email

Notes

Name

Address

Home Work

Cell Email

Notes

Name

Address

Home Work

Cell Email

Notes

Name

Address

Home Work

Cell Email

Notes

Name

Address

Home Work

Cell Email

Notes

Name

Address

Home Work

Cell Email

Notes

Name

Address

Home Work

Cell Email

Notes

Name

Address

Home Work

Cell Email

Notes

Name

Address

Home Work

Cell Email

Notes

Name

Address

Home Work

Cell Email

Notes

Name

Address

Home Work

Cell Email

Notes

Name

Address

Home Work

Cell Email

Notes

Name

Address

Home Work

Cell Email

Notes

Name

Address

Home Work

Cell Email

Notes

Name

Address

Home Work

Cell Email

Notes

Name

Address

Home Work

Cell Email

Notes

Name

Address

Home Work

Cell Email

Notes

Name

Address

Home Work

Cell Email

Notes

Name

Address

Home Work

Cell Email

Notes

Name

Address

Home Work

Cell Email

Notes

Name

Address

Home Work

Cell Email

Notes

Name

Address

Home Work

Cell Email

Notes

Name

Address

Home Work

Cell Email

Notes

Name

Address

Home Work

Cell Email

Notes

Name

Address

Home Work

Cell Email

Notes

Name

Address

Home Work

Cell Email

Notes

Name

Address

Home Work

Cell Email

Notes

Name

Address

Home Work

Cell Email

Notes

Name

Address

Home Work

Cell Email

Notes

Name

Address

Home Work

Cell Email

Notes

Name

Address

Home Work

Cell Email

Notes

Name

Address

Home Work

Cell Email

Notes

Printed in Great Britain
by Amazon